Sports Training

Ice Hockey

Jack Otten

Rigby

Ice Hockey
Copyright © 2001 by Rosen Book Works, Inc.

On Deck™ Reading Libraries
Published by Rigby
a division of Reed Elsevier Inc.
1000 Hart Road
Barrington, IL 60010-2627
www.rigby.com

Book Design: Sam Jordan
Text: Jack Otten
Photo Credits: Cover, pp. 4, 6–21 by Maura Boruchow;
p. 5 © Steve Babineau/AllSport

Thanks to Jaguars Ice Hockey Organization—Squirt B Team

06 05 04 03 02 01
10 9 8 7 6 5 4 3 2 1

Printed in The United States of America

ISBN 0-7635-7850-9

Contents

Introduction

Pavel Bure is a pro hockey player.
He is strong and fast on the ice.
The boys below want to be pro
hockey players someday.

Getting Ready

Hockey players wear ice skates and padded pants. Pads keep them safe. They also wear pads on their shoulders, elbows, and legs.

Ice Skates

Hockey players wear helmets. They wear padded gloves to protect their hands.

Helmet

Gloves

Warming Up

The coach helps the Wolves warm up. He tells two players to skate backward.

Backward

Skating backward is a skill players need. Skaters also need good balance. Good balance helps hockey players skate well.

The coach shows each player how to stop on skates. He tells the players to turn and dig their skates into the ice.

Dig In

Practicing Shots

The coach shows a player how to hit a puck. The players practice bending as they skate. This helps them keep their balance when they swing.

The coach tells a player to hit a slap shot. The player quickly pulls back his hockey stick.

He swings his stick hard at the puck. He hits the puck at the goal.

The coach tells the players to practice passing the puck.

The players face each other.
They hit the puck back and forth.

The Goalie

The goalie uses thick pads and a special stick. He wears a mask to protect his face.

Mask

Thick Pads

Wide Stick

The coach shows the goalie how to block a shot. The goalie stands in front of the goal. He bends his knees and holds his stick down.

The player hits the puck toward the goal. The puck comes in fast.

The goalie uses his stick to block the puck.

The Wolves play a practice game. The teams pass the puck. Players hit slap shots. The goalie blocks the shots.

The coach tells the team that they played well. They are becoming better players.

Glossary

goal (**gohl**) a metal frame with a net to catch pucks

goalie (**goh**-lee) a player who tries to keep the puck from entering the goal

practice (**prak**-tihs) to do something again and again to learn to do it well

pro (**proh**) an athlete who gets paid for playing his or her sport

puck (**puhk**) a round, flat rubber disk that is used in ice hockey

skate (**skayt**) to move on ice skates

slap shot (**slap shaht**) a shot made with a hard swinging stroke

warm up (**worm uhp**) to exercise before a game

Resources

Books

Kids' Book of Hockey: Skills, Strategies, Equipment, and the Rules of the Game
by John Sias
Transition Publishing (1997)

Hockey in Action
by Niki Walker
Crabtree Publishing (2000)

Web Site

All About Ice Hockey
http://members.aol.com/msdaizy/sports/
   hockey.html

Index